Coloring Book with Spac
Cosmos & Astronomy

LITERARY

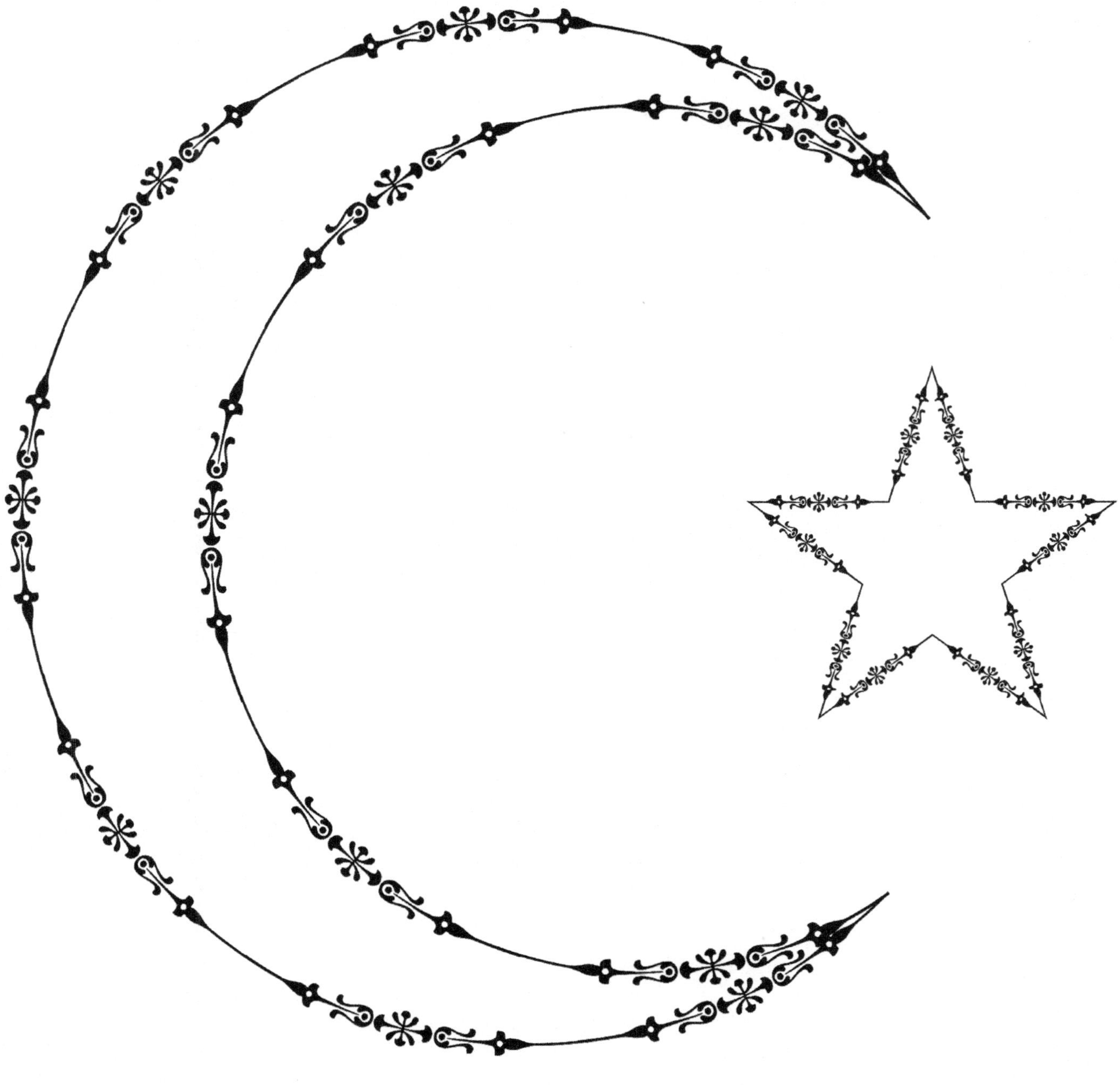

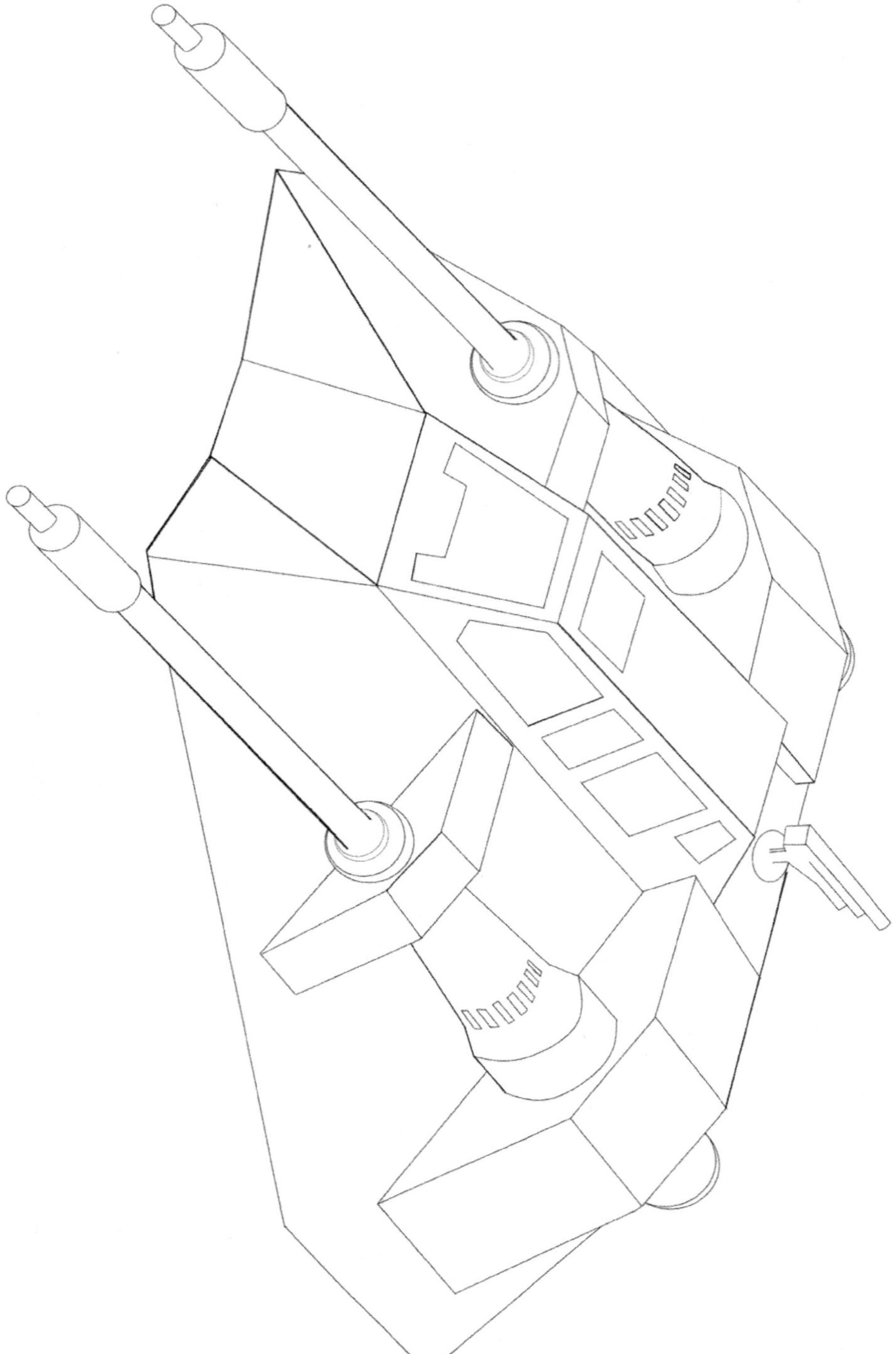

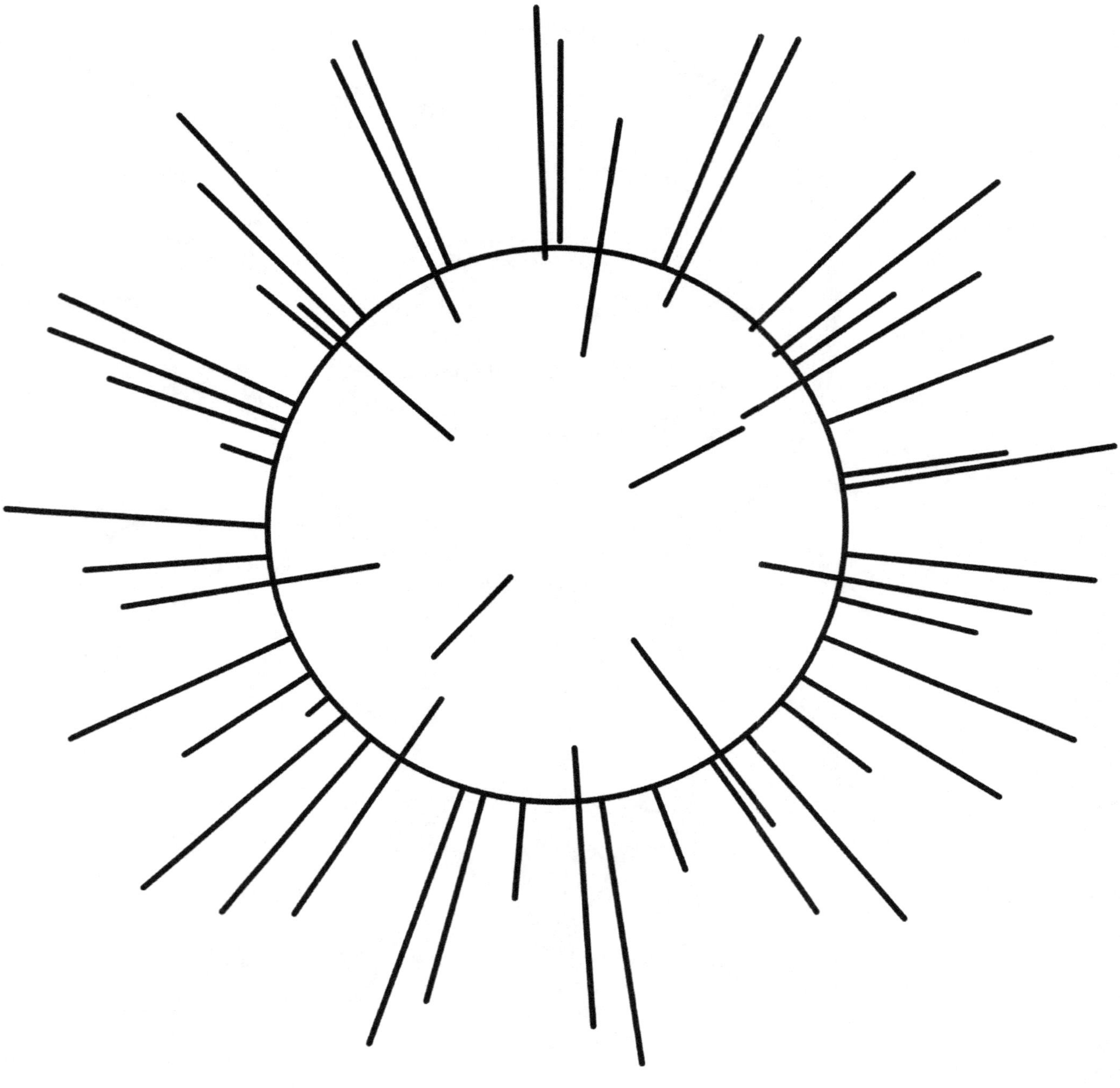

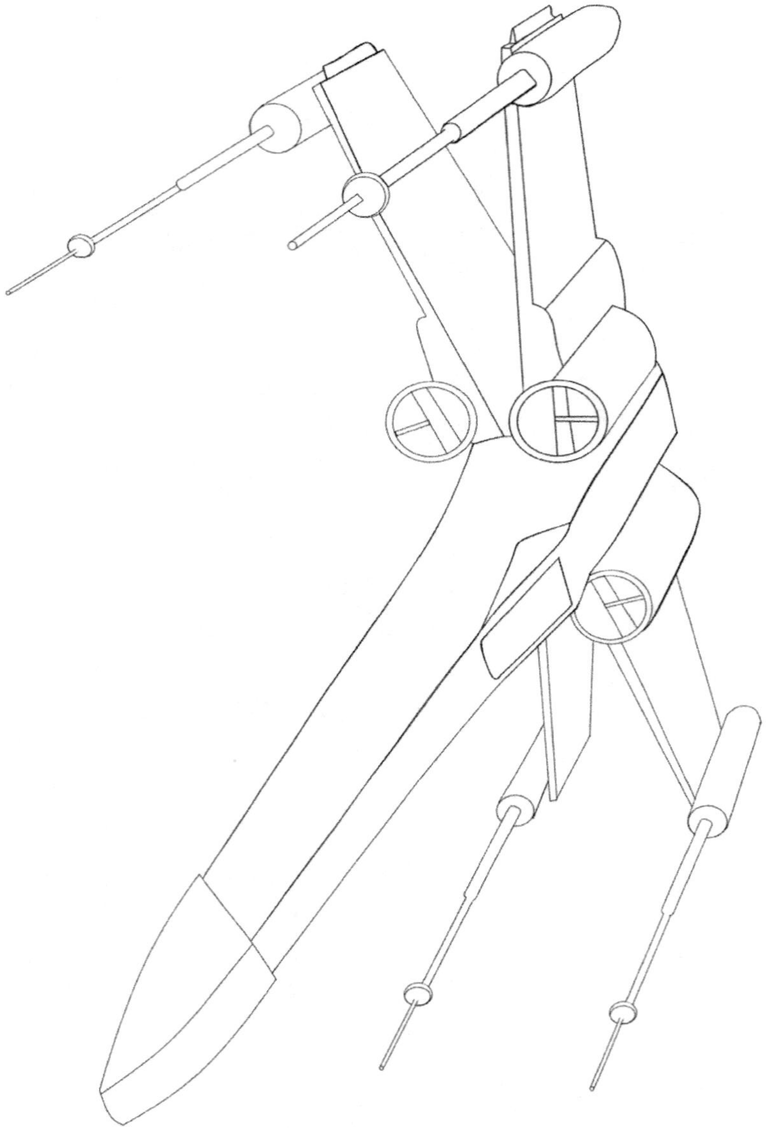

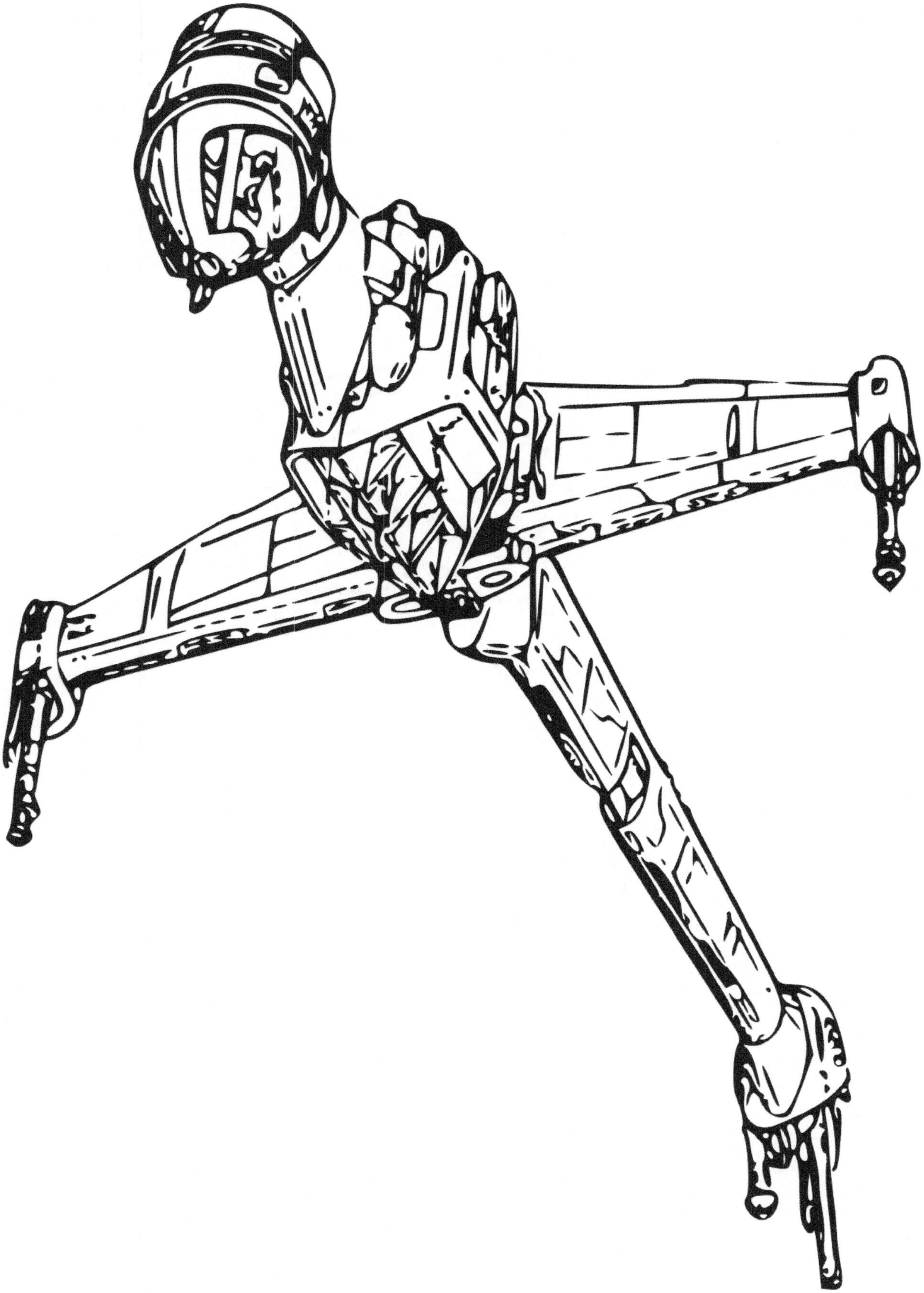

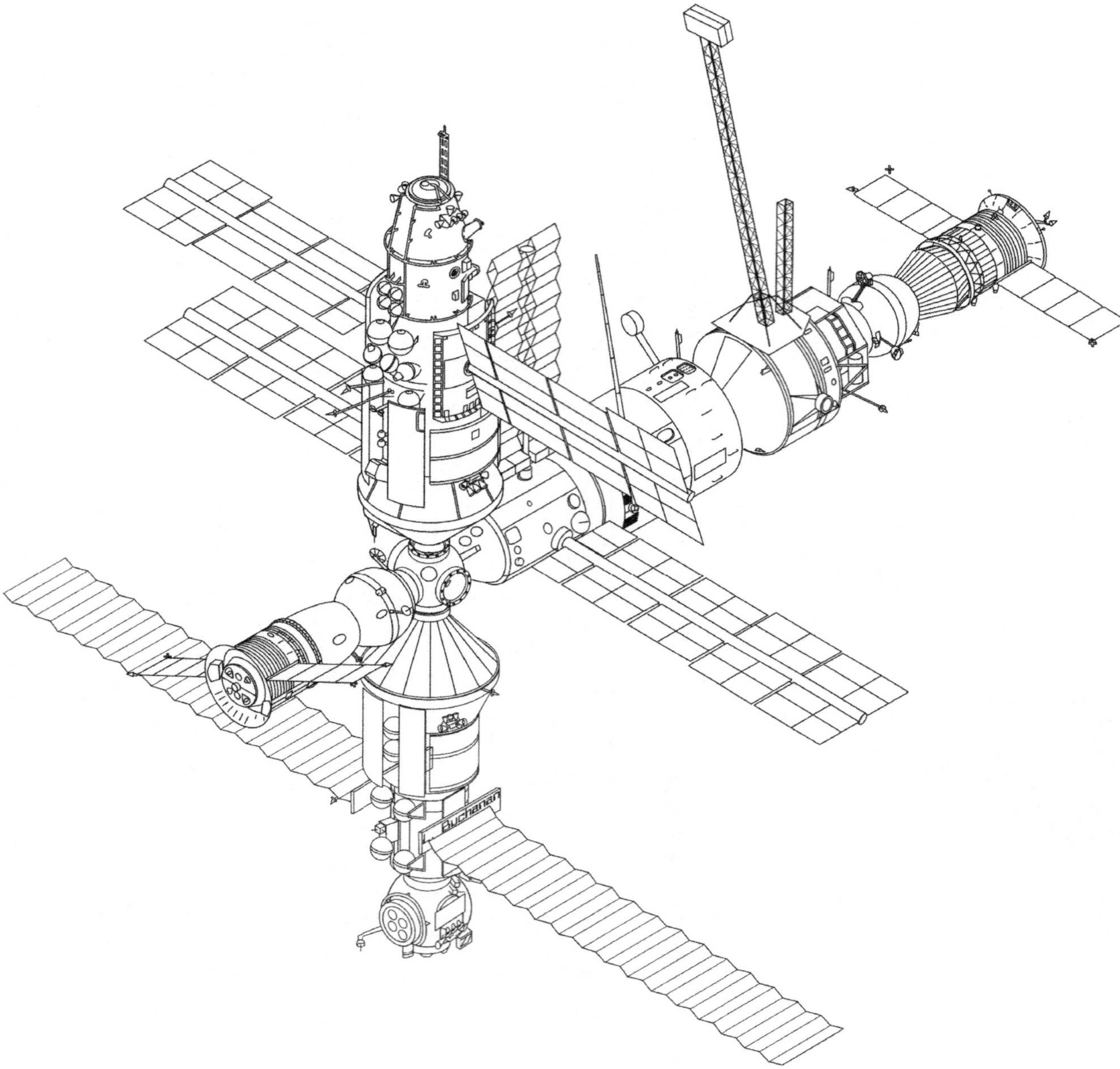
Buchanan

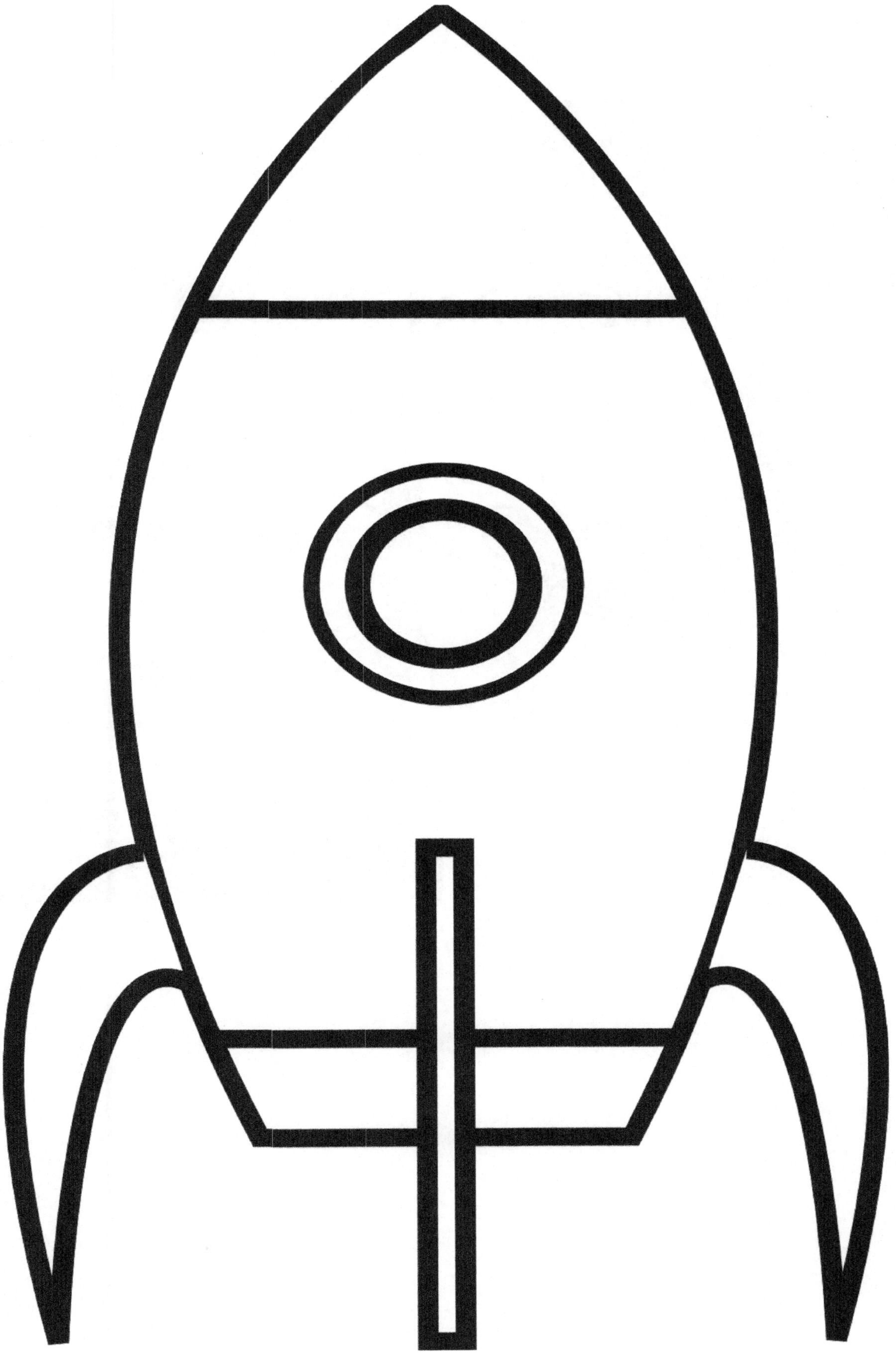

SPACE

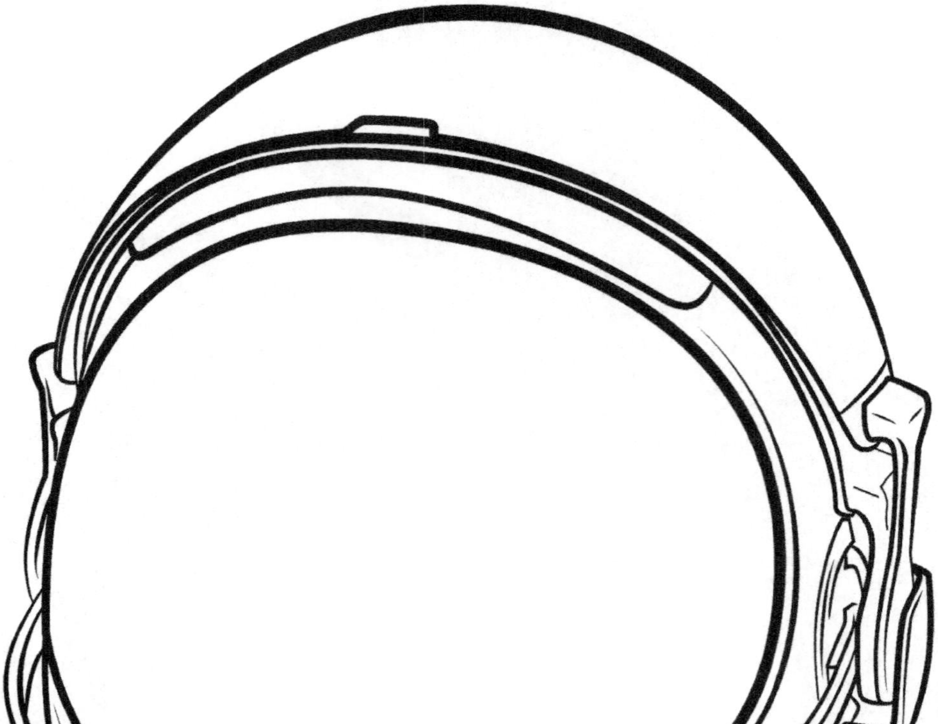

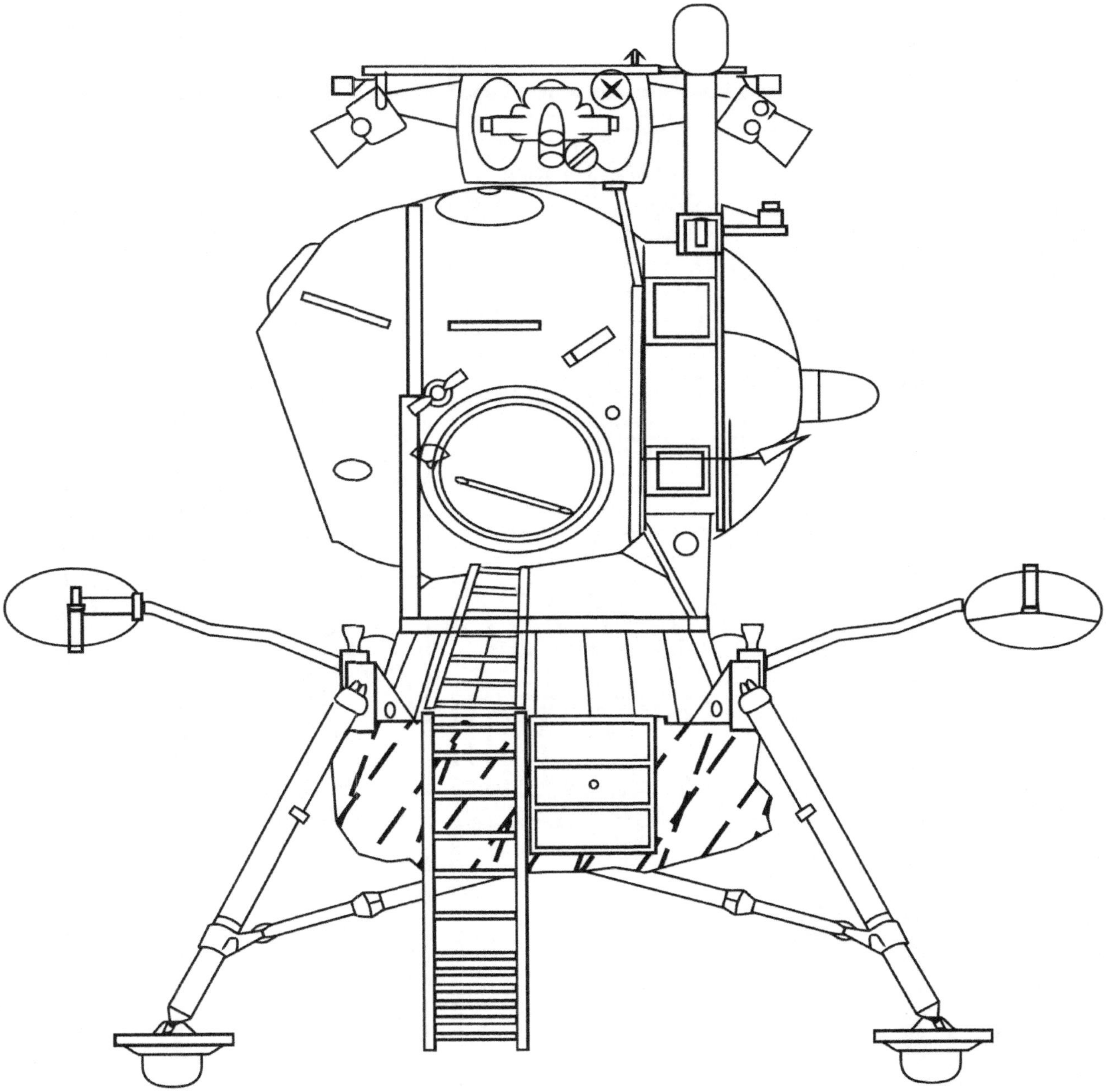

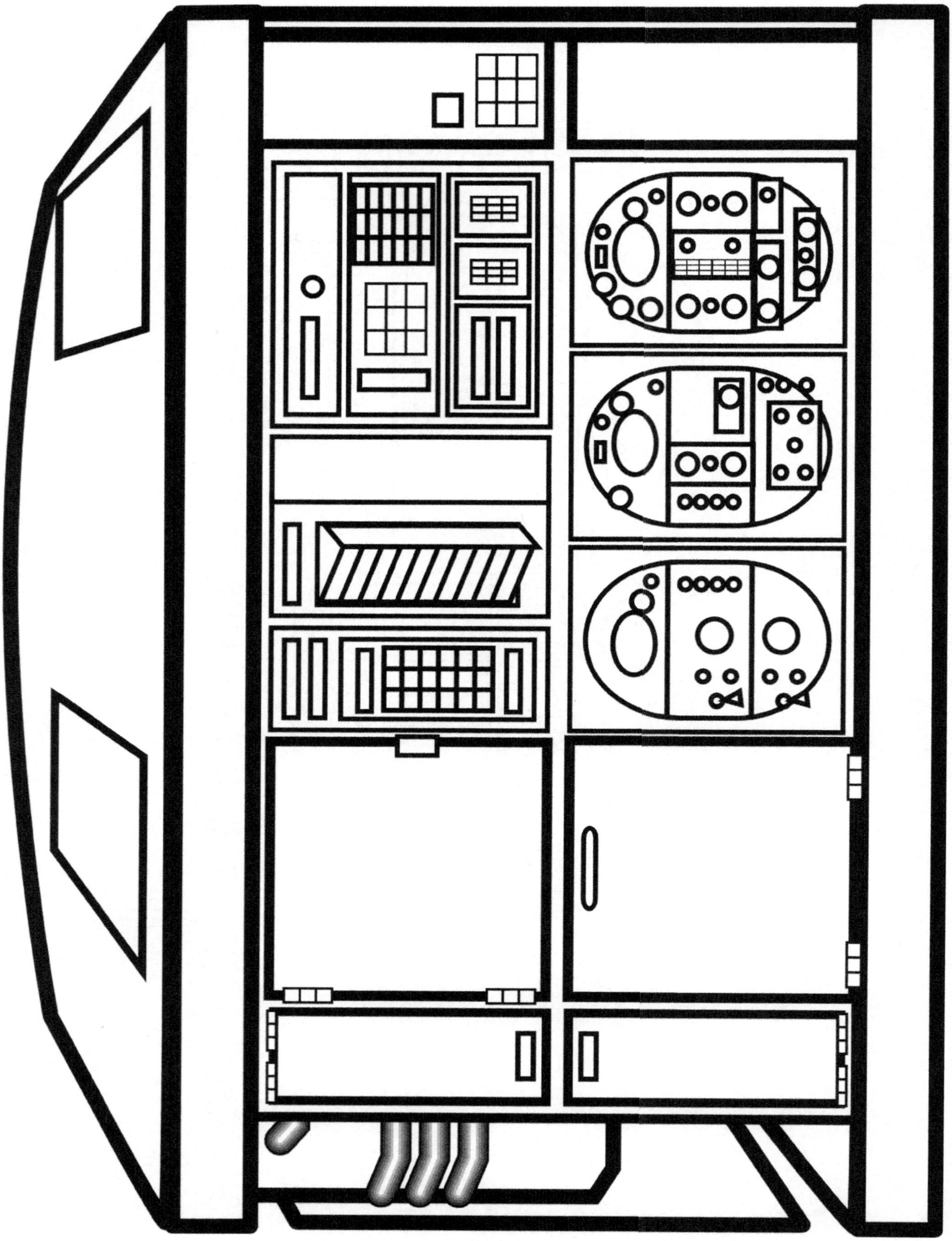

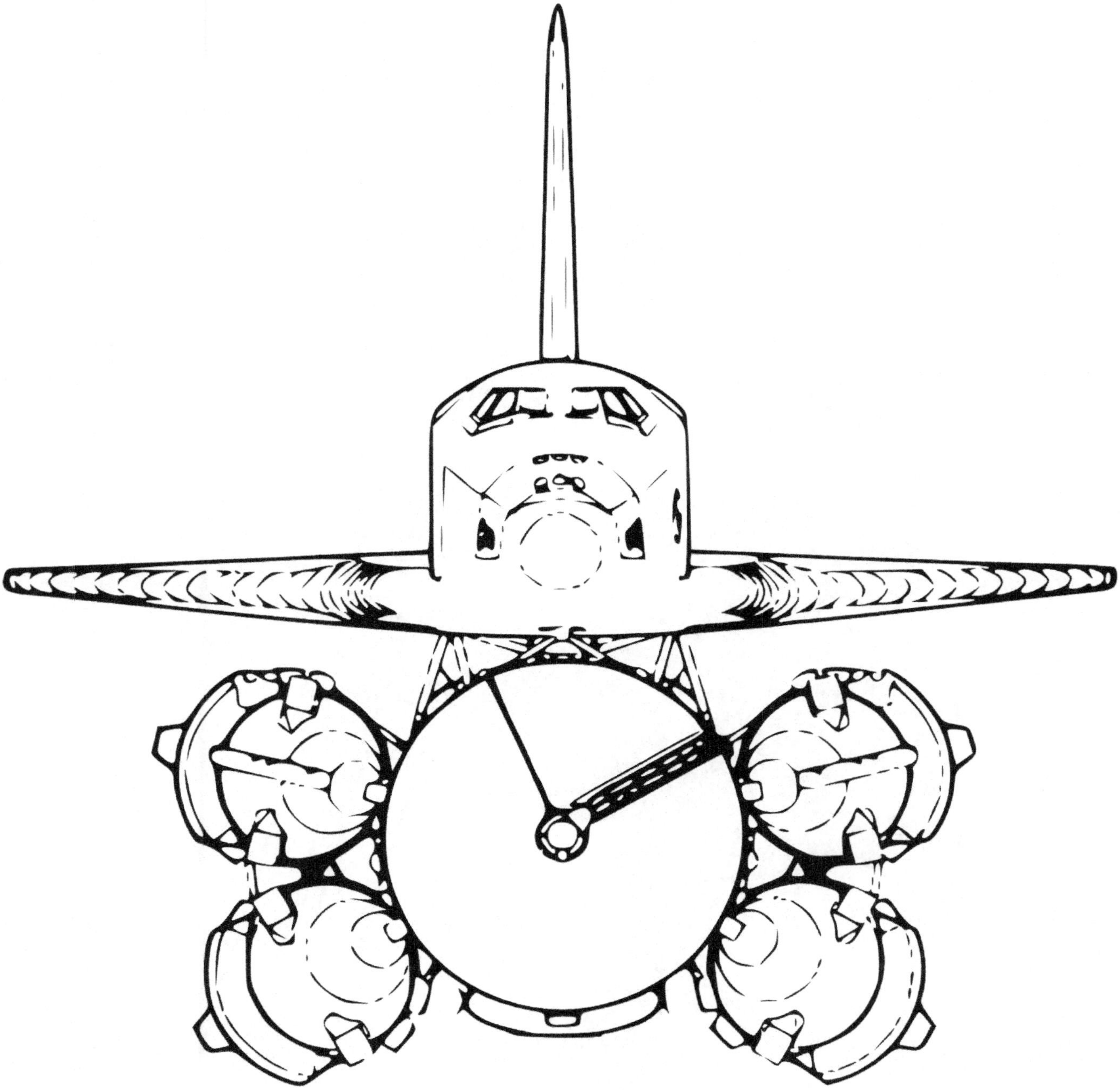

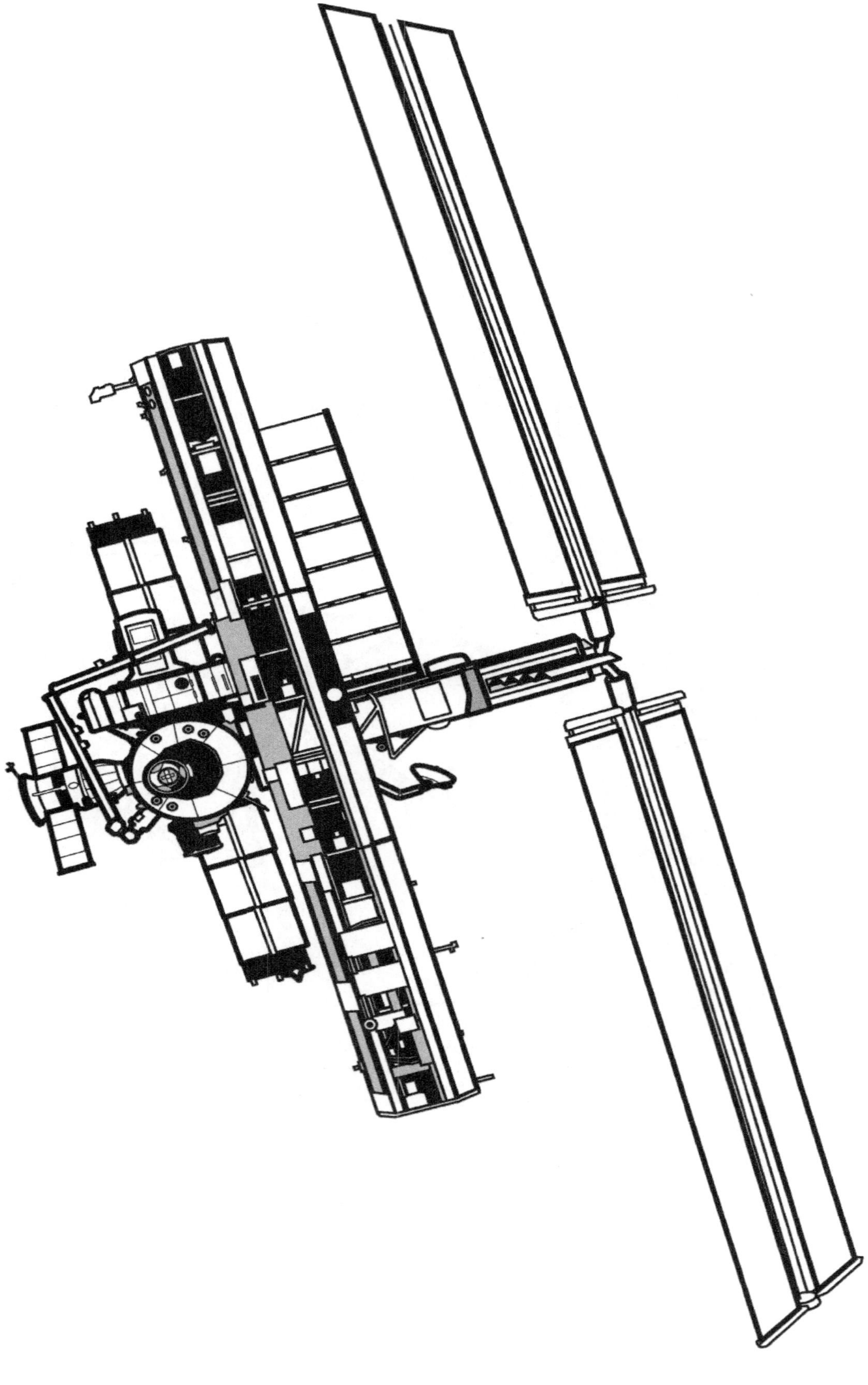

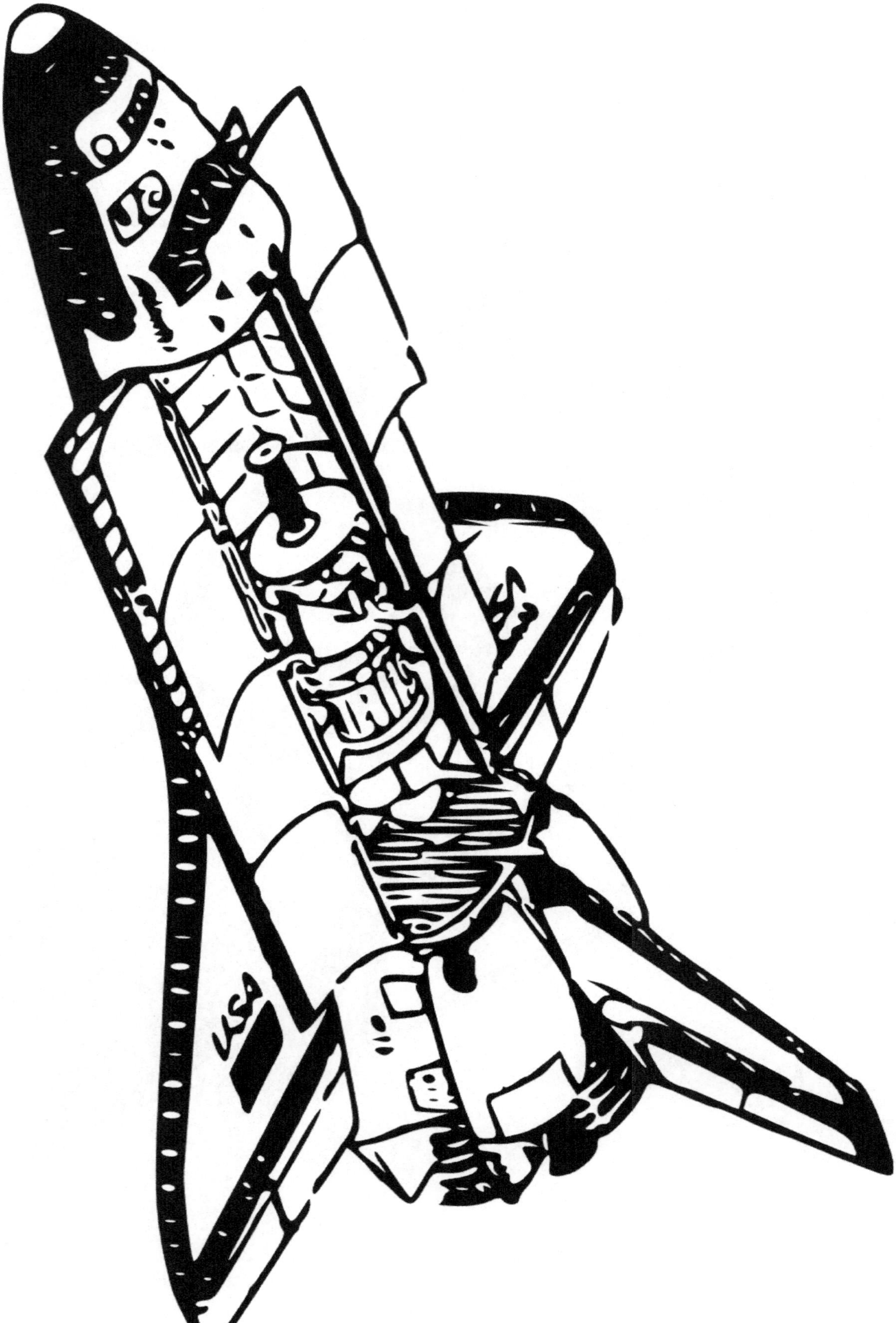
USA

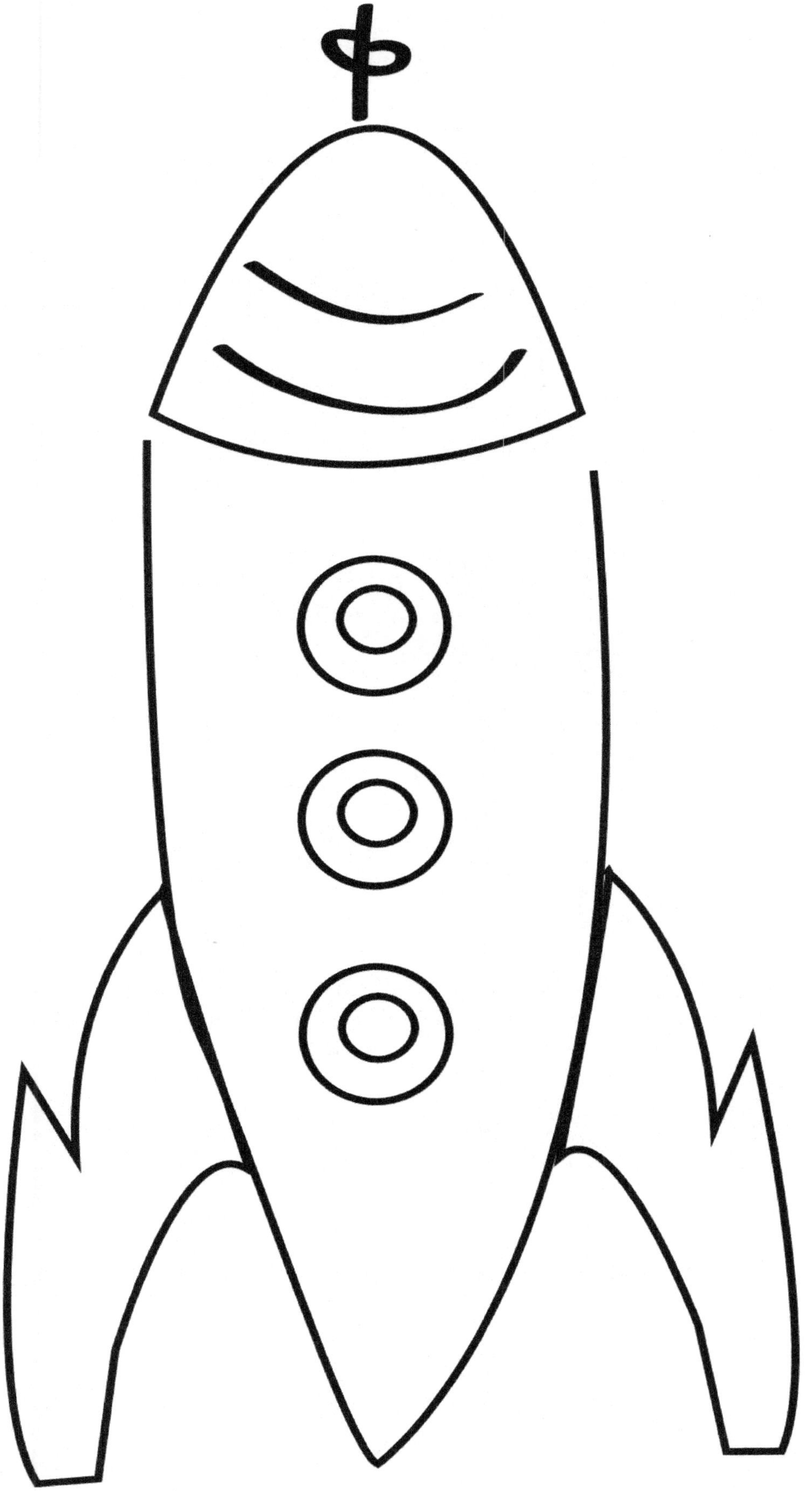

USA

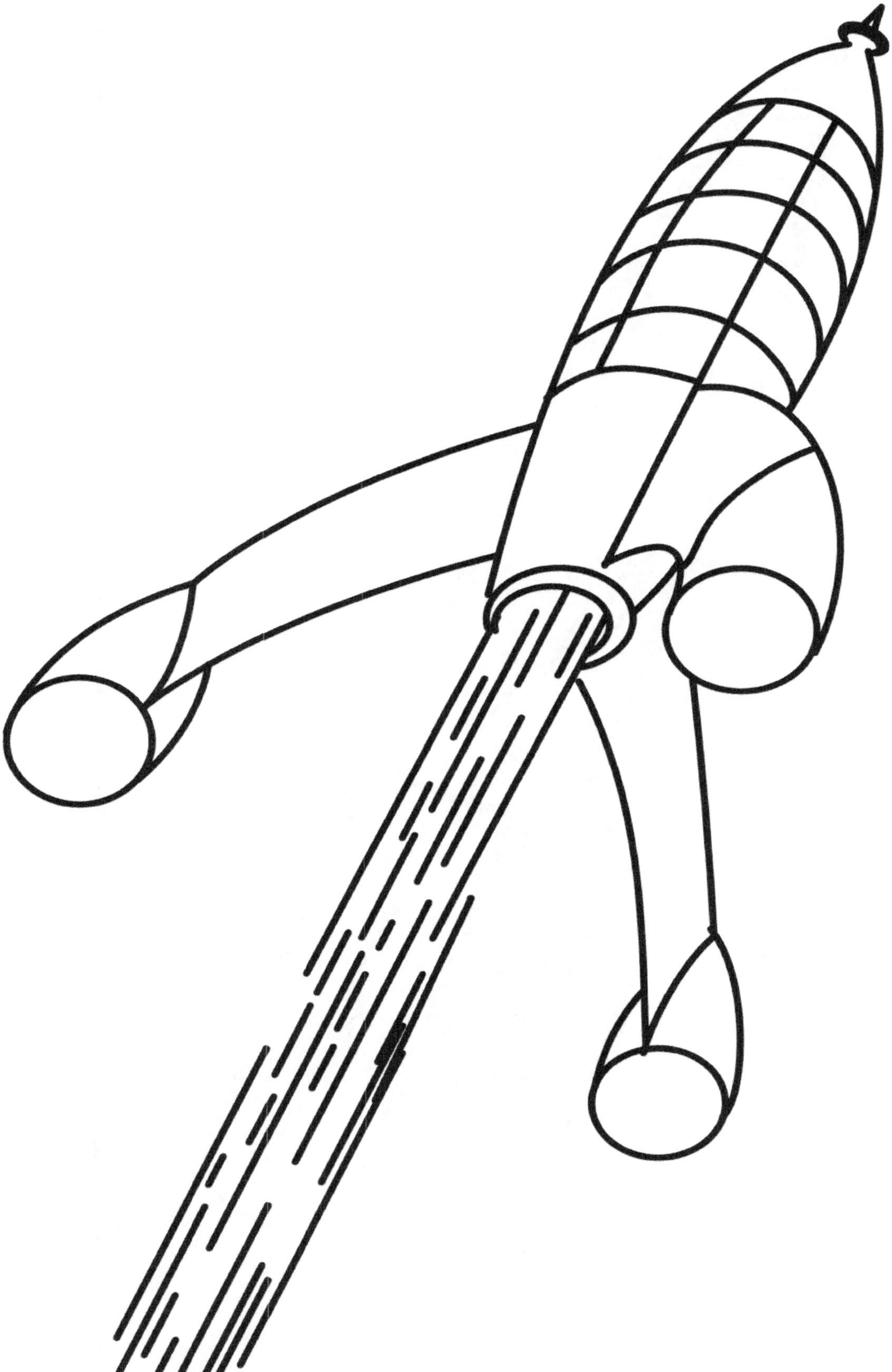

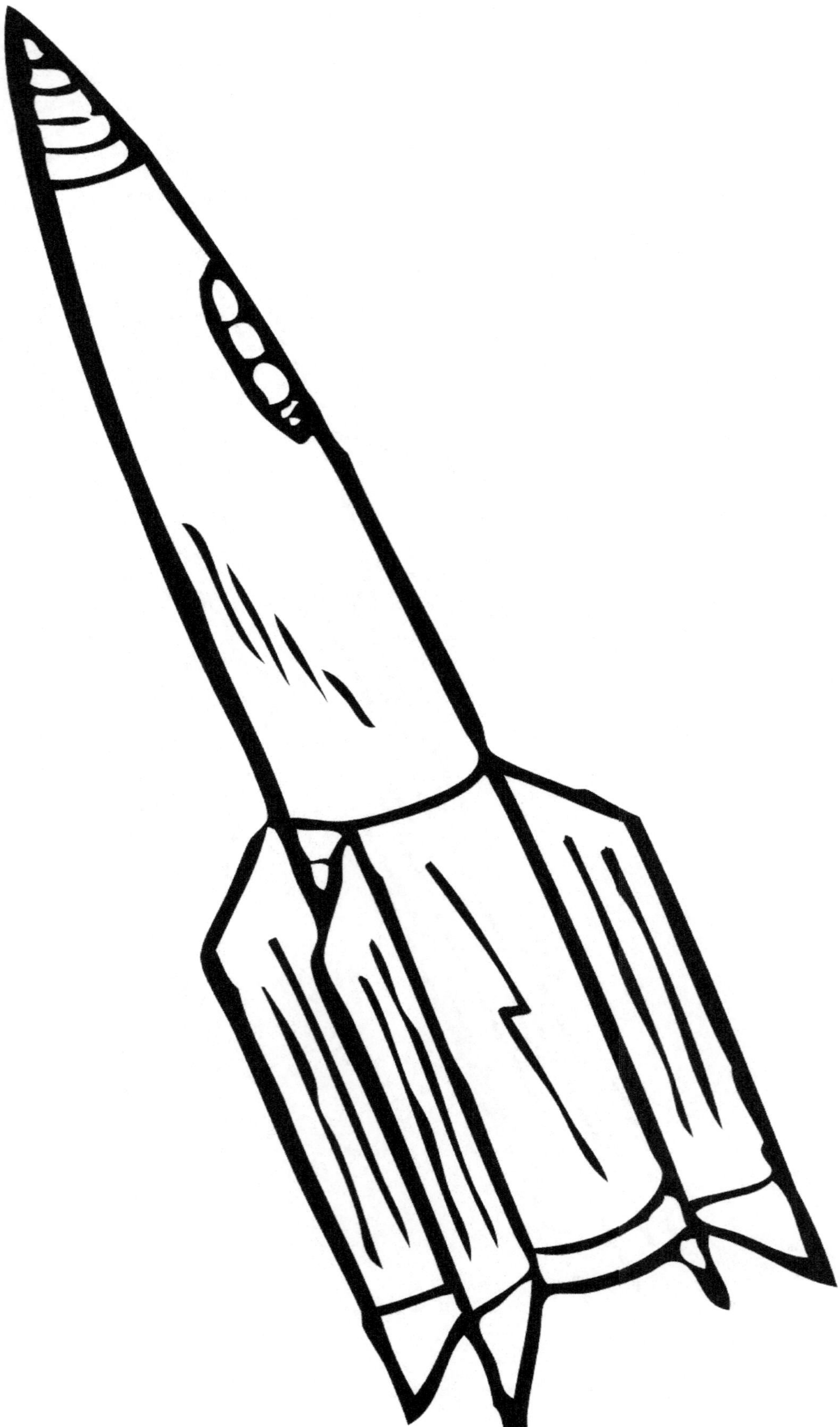

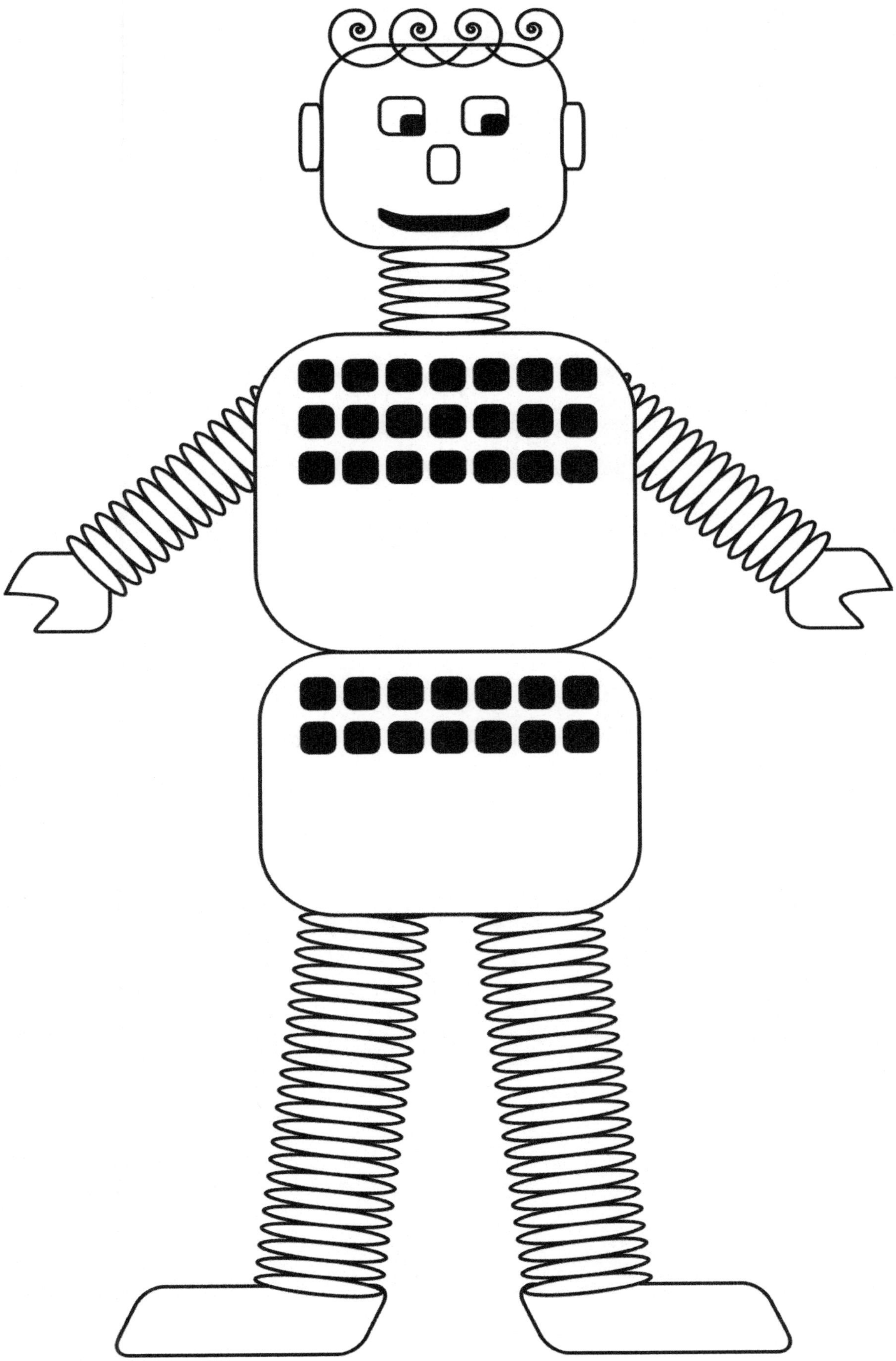

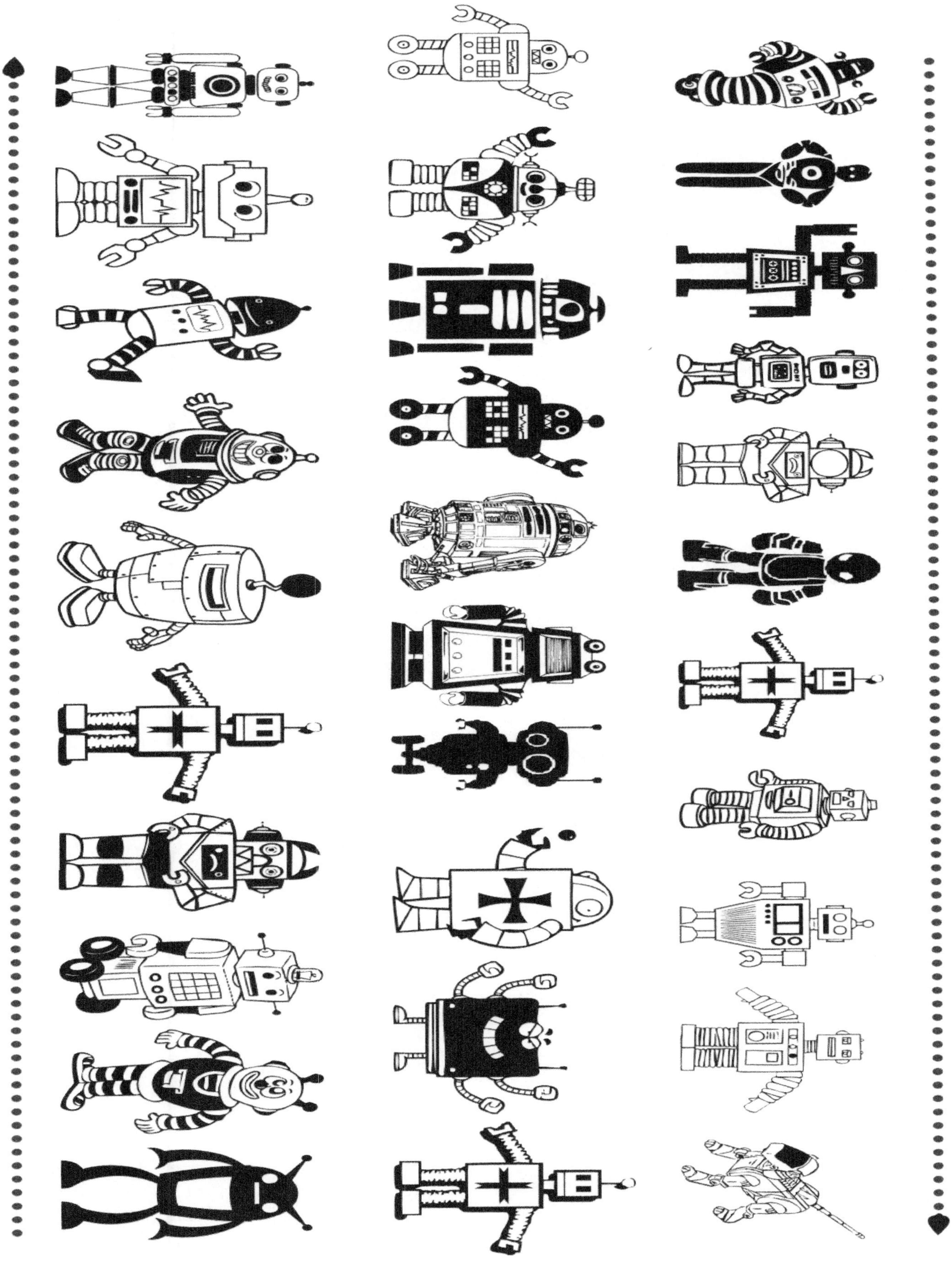

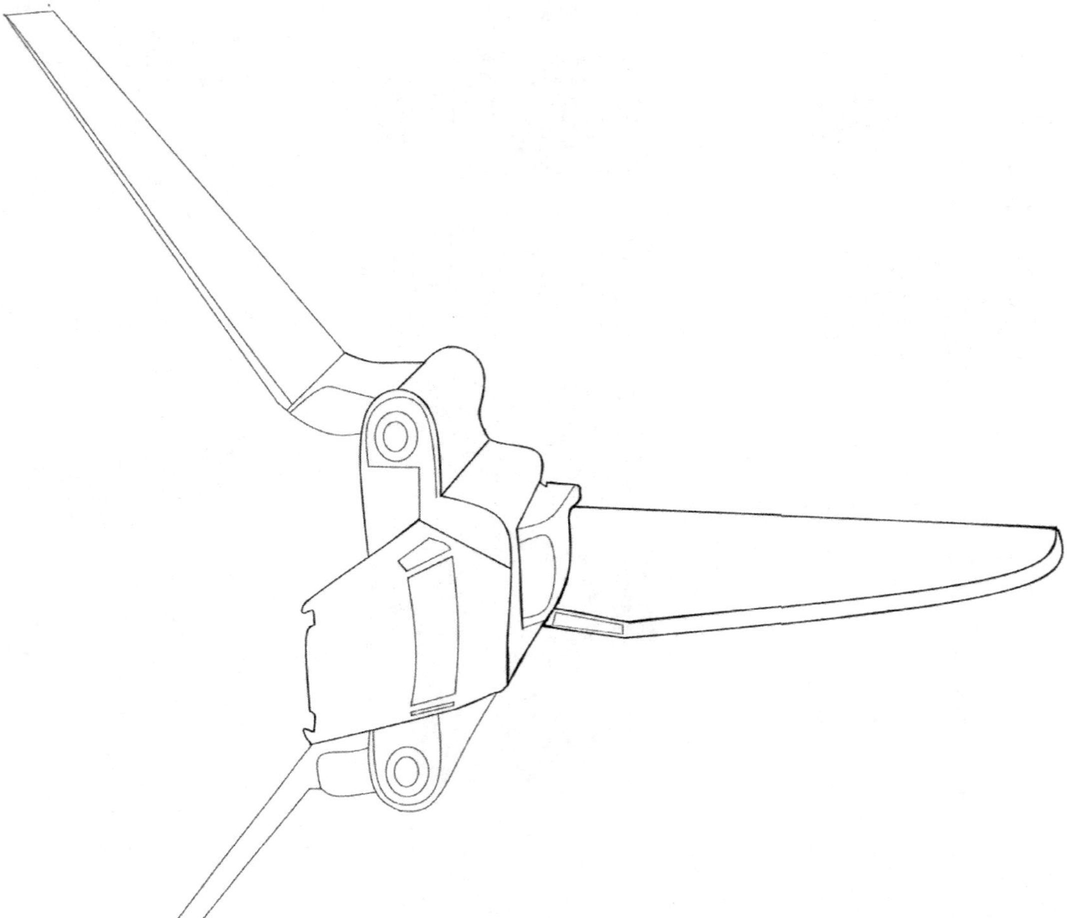

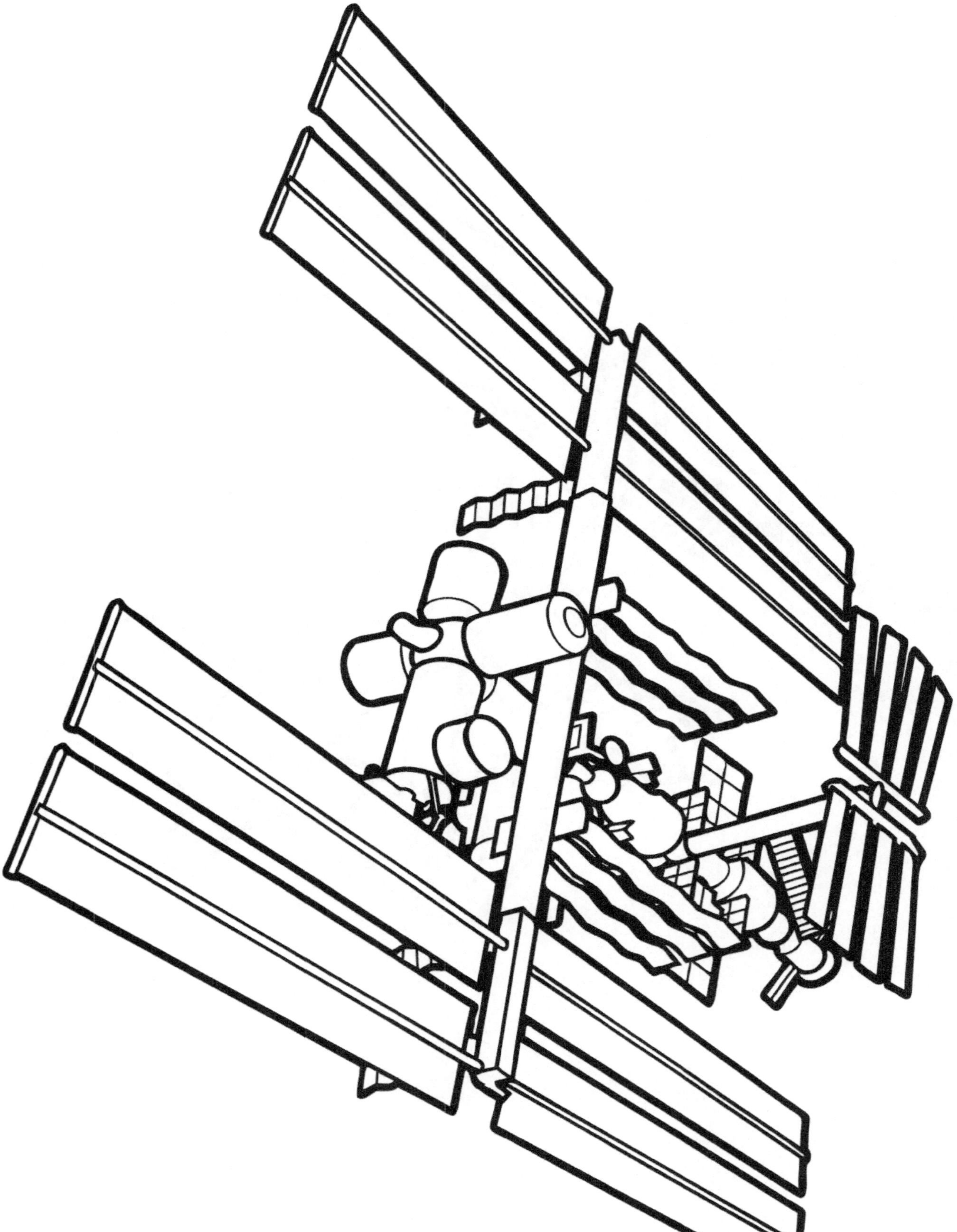

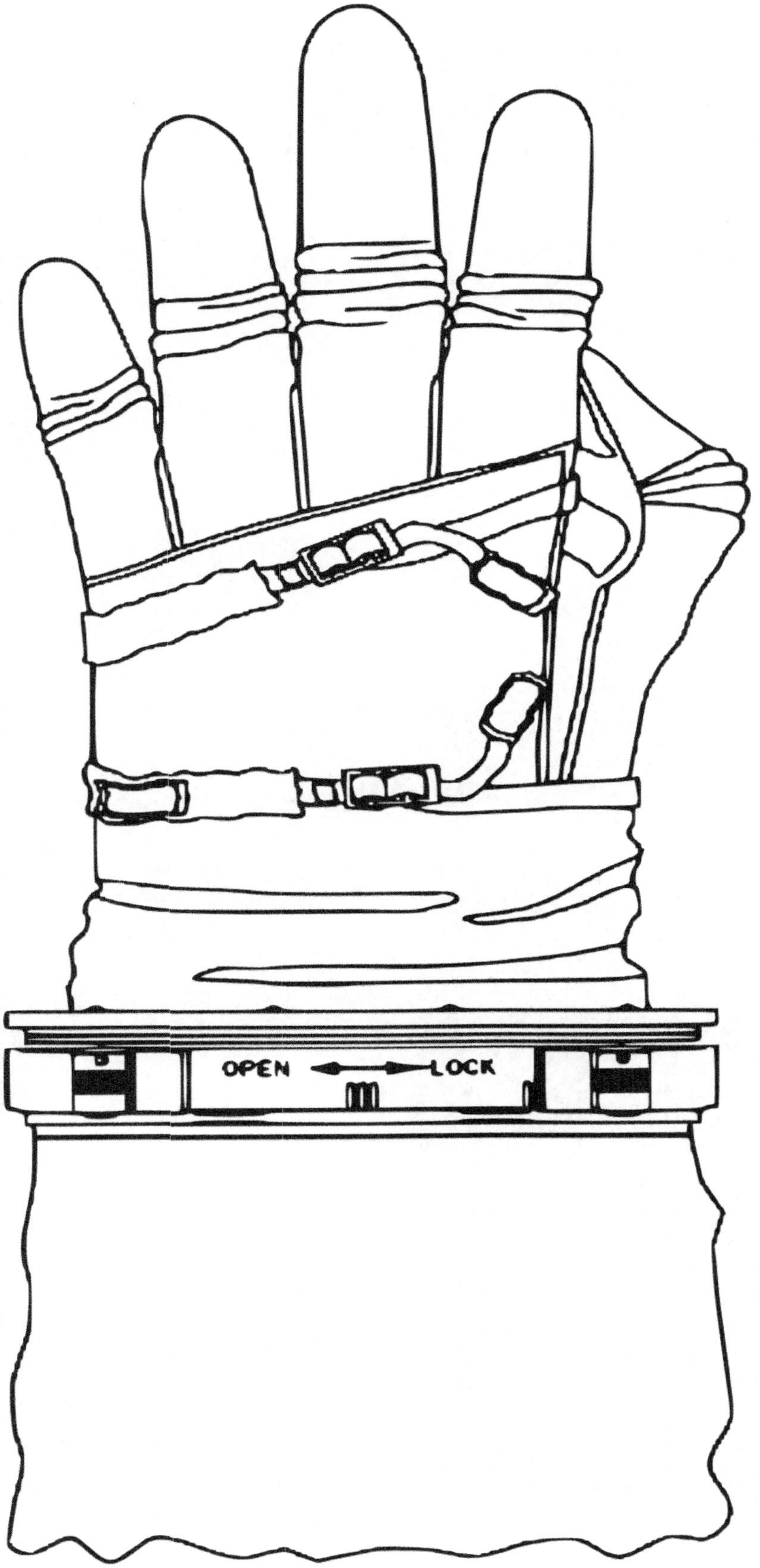
OPEN
LOCK

INK

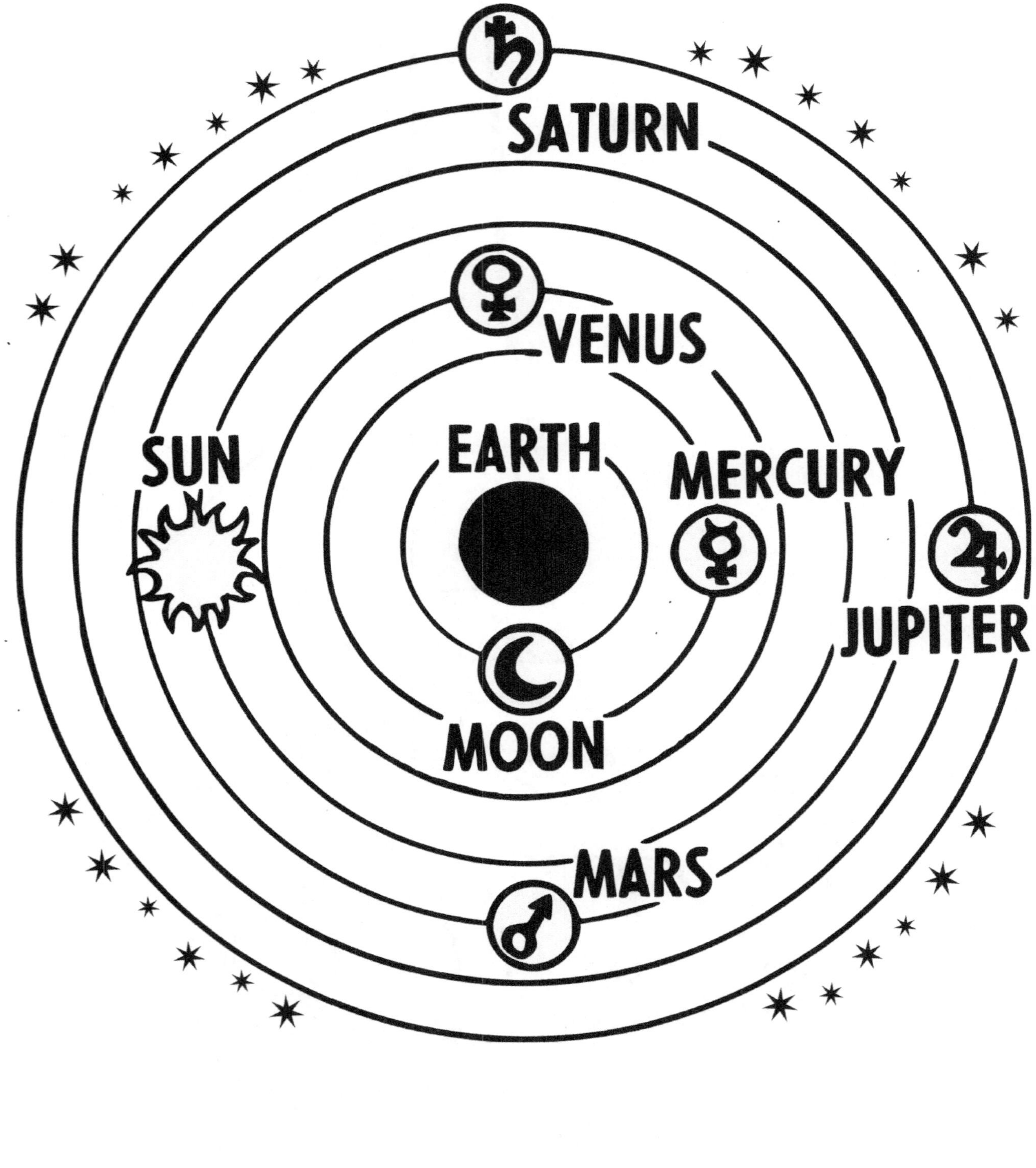
SATURN
VENUS
SUN
EARTH
MERCURY
JUPITER
MOON
MARS

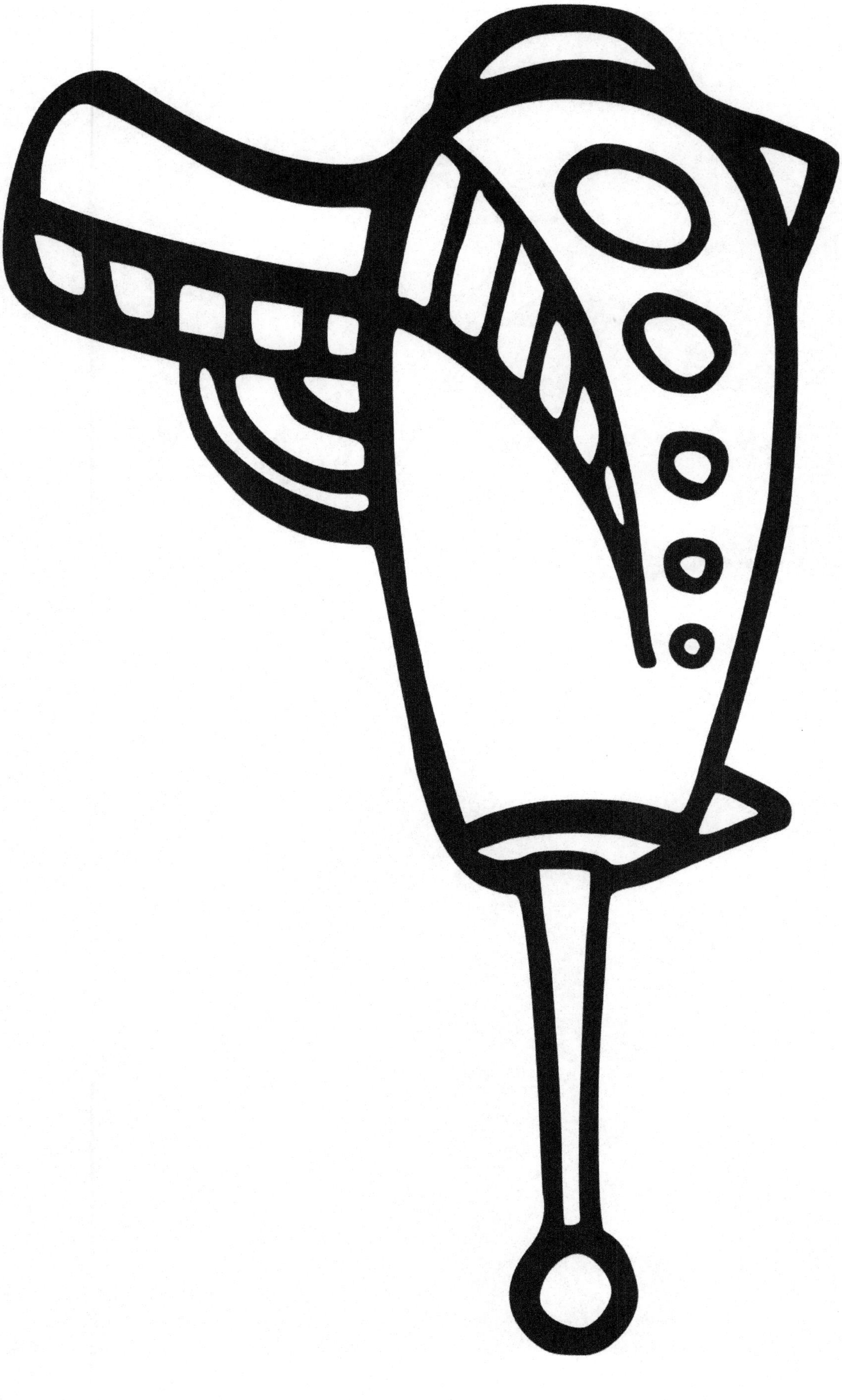

ZZZZZ

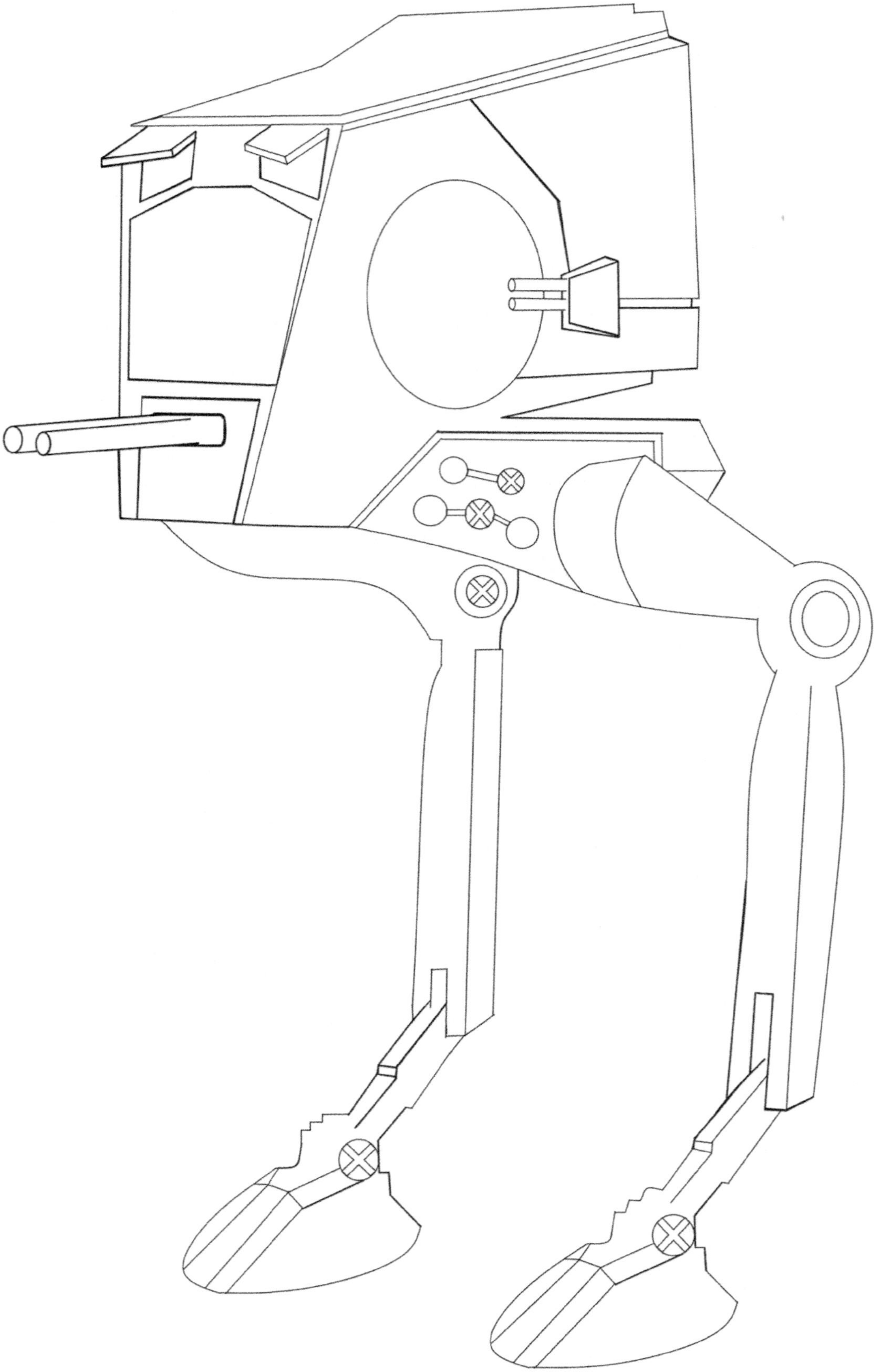

OZONE
LAYER

NASA

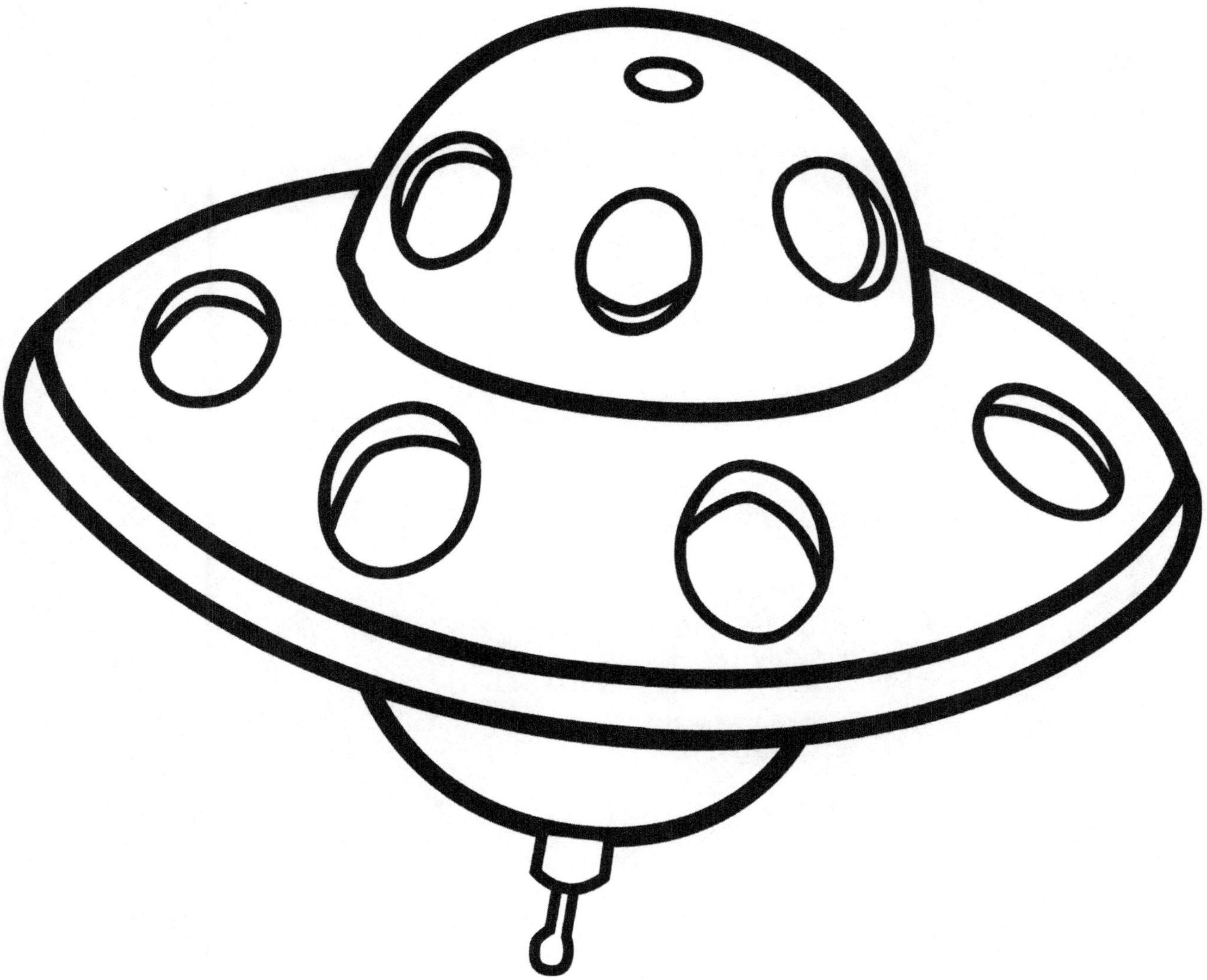

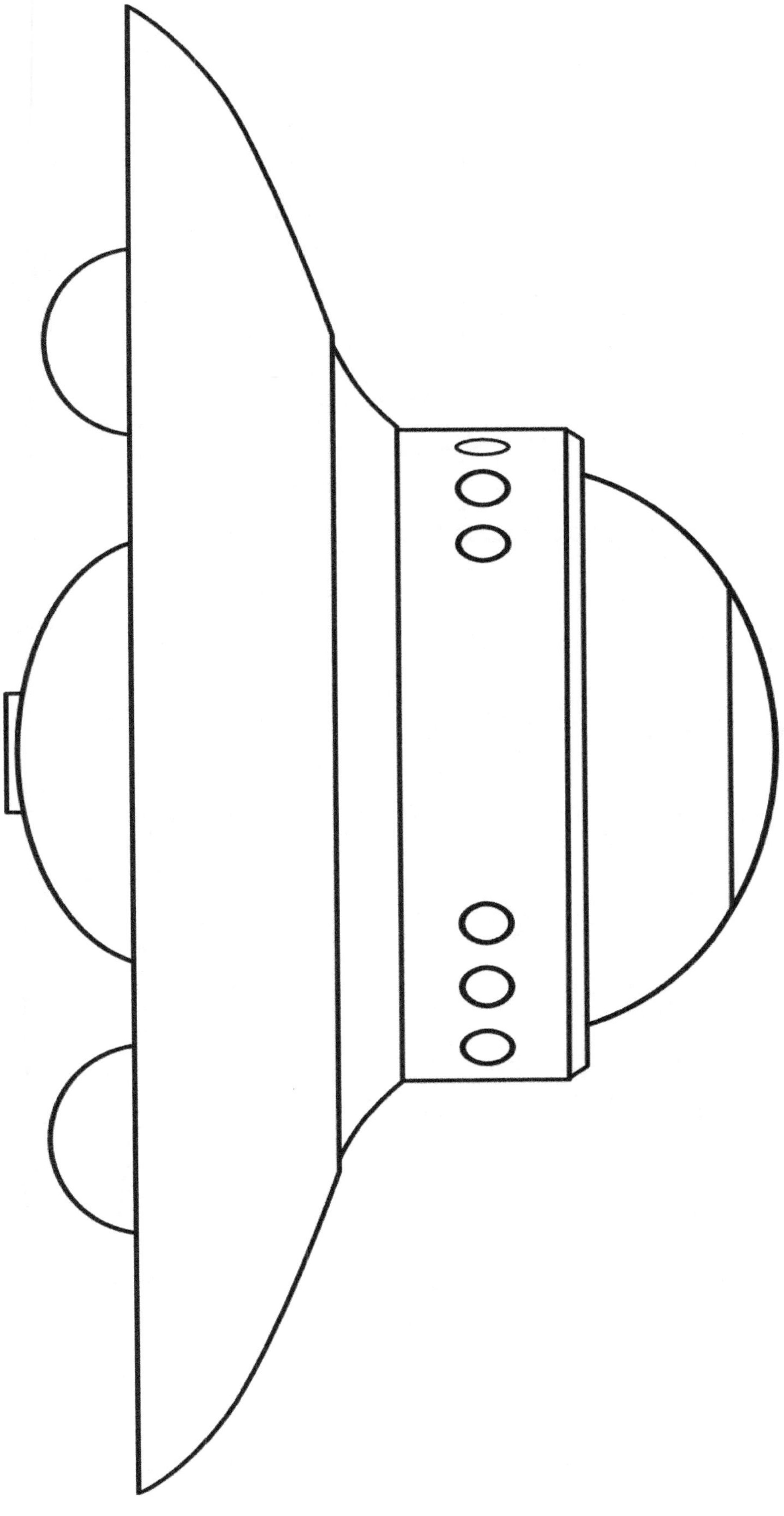

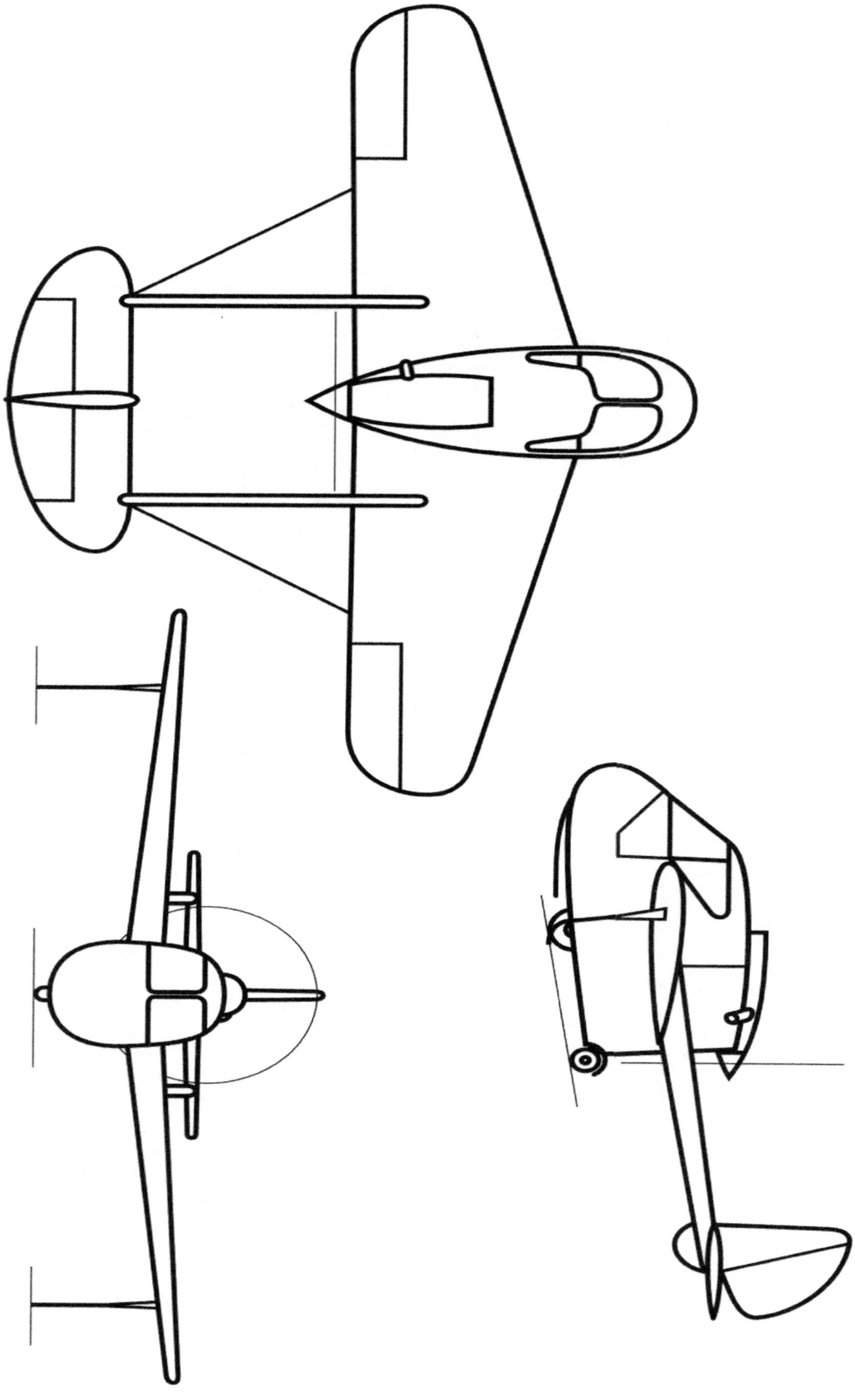

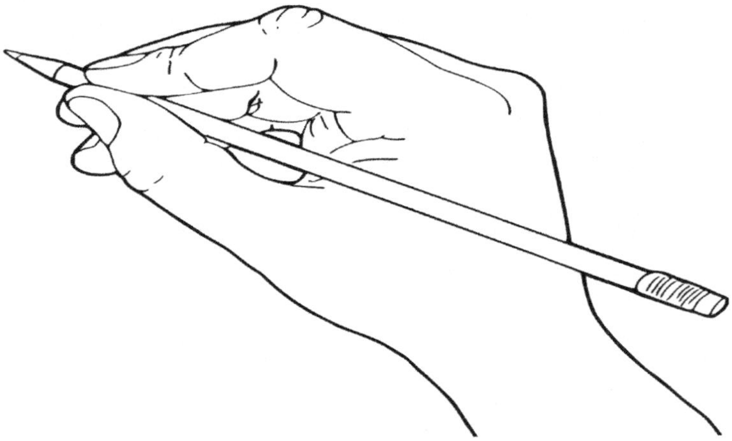

That's the END!

But keep on drawing & coloring and **learning every day!**

Printed in Great Britain
by Amazon

36721366R00031